9 Iguanas Itching on an Island

An ABC and Counting Book

By Robert and Ann Holmes
Illustrated by Sydney Holmes

Mind Skills 4 Kids • Santa Cruz

Mind Skills 4 Kids
PMB 337
1840 41st Avenue #102
Capitola, CA 95010

Visit our Web site at www.mindskills4kids.com
or email us at contactus@mindskills4kids.com

Library of Congress Control Number: 2006906695

ISBN-13: 978-0-9788017-0-0
ISBN-10: 0-9788017-0-9

Aa is 1

1 Alligator
Asleep on an Airplane

Bb is 2

2 Beavers

Bouncing on the Bed

Cc is 3

3 Cats
Cleaning the Closet

Dd is 4

4 Dinosaurs

Dancing Downstairs

Ee is 5

5 Elephants
Entering an Elevator

Ff is 6

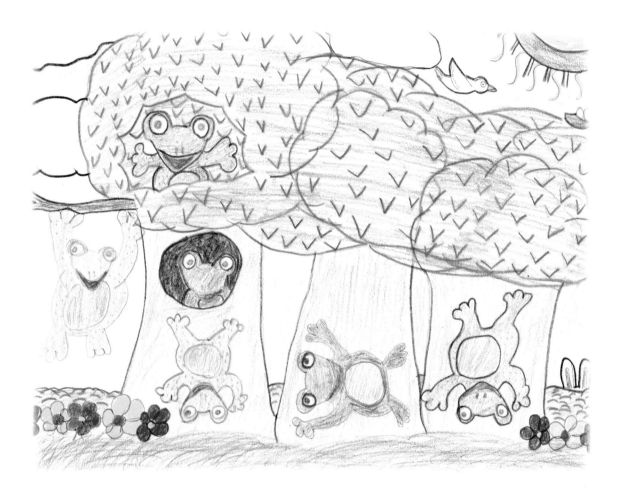

6 Frogs
Frolic in the Forest

Gg is 7

7 Geese
Gabbing in the Garden

Hh is 8

8 Hens

Hip Hop in the House

Ii is 9

9 Iguanas
Itching on an Island

Jj is 10

10 Jaguars
Jogging in the Jungle

Kk is 11

11 Kangaroos
Knit in the Kitchen

Ll is 12

12 Llamas

Lunching on the Lawn

Mm is 13

13 Monkeys

Marching in the Mall

Nn is 14

14 Newts
Nap at the Neighbors

Oo is 15

15 Otters
Occupy the Office

Pp is 16

16 Poodles

Pose on the Porch

Qq is 17

17 Quails
Quarrel in the Quarry

Rr is 18

18 Rabbits

Race on the Roof

Ss is 19

19 Squirrels
Singing in the Shower

Tt is 20

20 Turtles
Tricycle to Town

Uu is 21

21 Umbrella Birds
Unpack Upstairs

V v is 22

22 Viceroys

Visiting in the Village

Ww is 23

23 Woodchucks
Whistle in the Woods

Xx is 24

24 Xemas
Xing on the Xebec

Yy is 25

25 Yaks

Yelling in the Yard

Zz is 26

Zebra's Zipping Zone

26 Zebras
Zip Around the Zoo

GLOSSARY (What the words in the book mean)

Aa Alligator
Asleep – napping, resting, sleeping, snoozing
Airplane – aircraft, plane, jet, flying machine

Bb Beaver
Bounce – hop, jump, leap
Bed – cot, crib, bunk

Cc Cat
Cleaning – wash, clean, polish
Closet – small room, cupboard, locker

Dd Dinosaur
Dancing – hop, spin, whirl
Downstairs – lower floor

Ee Elephant
Entering – go in
Elevator – machine that carries things up and down

Ff Frog
Frolic – play, sport, have fun
Forest – woods, woodland, grove of trees

Gg Geese
Gabbing – talk, chatter, gossip
Garden – yard, plants, farm

Hh Hen
Hip Hop – jump, skip, bound, twirl
House – home, shelter, abode

Ii Iguana
Itching – scratching
Island – land surrounded by water

Jj Jaguar
Jogging – run, trot
Jungle – woods, rain forest, overgrown woods

Kk Kangaroo
Knit – make cloth with needles and yarn
Kitchen – a room where food is cooked

Ll Llama
Lunching – eating lunch
Lawn – grass, yard

Mm Monkey
Marching – walk, parade
Mall – stores, shops, markets

Nn Newt
Nap – a short sleep
Neighbors – person next door

Oo Otter

Occupy – live, fill, dwell
Office – a room where people work

Pp Poodle

Pose – way of holding the body, hold a position
Porch – covered way into a building

Qq Quail

Quarrel – argue, have words, blow up
Quarry – dig, mine, pit

Rr Rabbit

Race – run, hurry, speed
Roof – cover, top, ceiling

Ss Squirrel

Singing – make music with the voice
Shower – bath water pours down from above

Tt Turtle

Tricycle – three-wheel cart that works with pedals
Town – city, village

Uu Umbrella Bird

Unpack – take things out of
Upstairs – up the stairs, on an upper floor

Vv Viceroy (a kind of butterfly)

Visiting – go to see, come to see

Village – a small city or a small town

Ww Woodchuck

Whistle – make a clear high sound with your lips

Woods – trees, forest

Xx Xema (said "zee mah") a seagull of the artic

Xing – crossing

Xebec – (say "zee beck") a small ship with 3 sails

Yy Yak

Yelling – scream, shout

Yard – piece of ground around a house

Zz Zebra

Zip – move with great energy

Zoo – place where wild animals are kept and shown